WHEN CROCODILES CRY
365 MORE Amazing Facts About The Animal Kingdom

Sally Meadows

Copyright © 2019 by Sally Meadows
https://sallymeadows.com

All rights reserved. No part of this book may be reproduced or transmitted in any form or by any means, electronic or mechanical, including photocopying, recording, or by any information storage and retrieval system, without permission in writing from the publisher.

ISBN: 978-1-988983-08-0

Published by Siretona Creative, Calgary, AB
www.siretona.com

Cover Design: Ellen Hooge
Interior Design: Colleen McCubbin and Ellen Hooge

COVER PHOTOS AND CLIPART

Photo licence: Creative Commons Attribution 2.0 Generic (CC BY 2.0)
https://openclipart.org

Contents

Introduction	5
Eye Openers	7
All the Sounds	13
All the Smells	17
Come Here My Sweet	20
Lickety-Split	25
Out It Comes	27
Going the Distance	31
The Bad and the Good	35
Dancing Fools	37
Covert Operations	41
Colour My World	46
Oh Baby!	51
Water Tales	59
Community	64
Helping Humans	69
Creative/Intelligent	73
Flip Flop	76
More Than Skin Deep	79
Tongues, Mouths, & Teeth	83
If Trees Could Talk	87
Toxin Tales	91
By the Numbers	95
That's Just Not Right	99
You Can't Make This Stuff Up	104
Questions	114
Answers	117
Author's Note	119

INTRODUCTION

The animal kingdom is full of delightful creatures that are simply amazing! I have spent hundreds of hours researching all kinds of media to find the most astonishing facts about animals to include in this second book in the series, just for you! I hope what you learn makes you gasp and giggle as much as I did!

Whether for the home, school, or public library, this book is perfect for anyone and everyone who is curious about the wonderful world of animals. As a bonus, you can download FREE extension activity worksheets for each book in the series at https://sallymeadows.com/free-stuff.

Use these fun facts as a starting point to do your own research on the amazing animal kingdom! Enjoy!

Sally Meadows

EYE OPENERS

1 The web-footed gecko quenches its thirst by licking moisture from its eyeballs.

2 The box jellyfish has 24 eyes.

3 A guinea pig sleeps with its eyes open.

EYE OPENERS

4 The yellow mongoose has rectangular pupils.

5 The stargazer (fish) has eyes on top of its head that shoot out electricity to stun its prey.

6 An ostrich's eyes are bigger than its brain.

7 A polar bear has a membrane over each eye that helps protect them from the sun's harmful ultraviolet light.

EYE OPENERS

8) The chiton mollusk has thousands of eyes, made of minerals, embedded in its skin.

9) The male stalk-eyed fly has an eye at the end of each of two stalks sticking out from the sides of his head. During mating season, he stands eyeball-to-eyeball with other males. The male with the biggest distance between his eyes—and the longest eyestalks—wins the female.

10) Cats, dogs, and horses can have heterochromia—two different-coloured eyes.

EYE OPENERS

11 The four-eyed fish has two eyes with two pupils each. When it floats at the surface of the water, the upper half of its eyes is above water watching out for predators, while the bottom half is under water looking for prey.

12 The compound eyes of a dragonfly, which have up to 30,000 facets each, give it excellent vision. It's one of the reasons why it is one of the most successful hunters in the animal kingdom.

13 The pot-bellied seahorse has eyes that move separately from one another, allowing it to look in two different directions at the same time.

EYE OPENERS

14 A bullfrog has see-through eyelids that slide over its eyes when it dives underwater to help protect them from floating debris.

15 Luminous bacteria behind the retinas of flashlight fish give them glowing eyes that they can blink on to attract prey, or blink off to avoid predators.

16 The dark patches around a meerkat's eyes help reduce glare from the sun so it has a better chance of spotting a predator.

17 Colour blindness is more common in male monkeys than female— same as for humans.

EYE OPENERS

18 The mystery snail, which has an eye at the end of each of two eyestalks, is able to regrow its eye if a stalk is cut off.

19 Shark corneas, which are similar to human corneas, have been used in human eye surgeries.

ALL THE SOUNDS

20 Songbirds babble before they are able to sing, similar to how human toddlers babble before they learn to talk.

21 When a virgin queen bee comes out of her pupa, she makes a piping or tooting sound to announce her arrival.

22 The blue whale can make a sound so thunderous that it sounds like the twin booster rockets of a space shuttle during liftoff.

ALL THE SOUNDS

23 During courting season, the male club-winged manakin (bird) creates chirping sounds by vibrating special club-shaped feathers.

24 To claim his territory and attract a female, the male orangutan barks, roars, sighs, and groans.

25 To protect itself from predators, the burrowing owl, which nests in an abandoned prairie dog burrow, makes a sound like a rattlesnake's rattle.

26 The ant nest beetle, which eats ants and their larvae, mimics the sound of an ant queen so it can gain access to the ants' nest.

27 When ready to mate, the male kakapo (bird) inflates its chest and releases a booming sound that can go on for eight hours a night, for up to eight months.

28 A male Madagascar hissing cockroach makes three different kinds of hissing sounds: to sound an alarm, when fighting with another male, and to attract a female.

29 When warning another animal (or human) to keep away, the brushtail possum makes a sound like a car that refuses to start.

ALL THE SOUNDS

30 The howler monkey is the loudest land animal with a call that can be heard up to 5 km (3 mi) away.

31 The loudest animal in the world for its size (1.3 cm; 0.5 in) is the water boatman. It makes a sound as loud as a diesel truck but because it lives in the water, most of the sound is muffled.

ALL THE SMELLS

32 The South American hoatzin is known as the "stink bird" because of the manure-smelling gas it releases while digesting its food.

33 During mating season, the male ring-tailed lemur rubs his tail against his stinky wrist and shoulder glands then waves it around to warn off other males.

34 When a caribou feels threatened, it rises up on its back legs and releases a scent from its ankles that warns other caribou about the danger.

ALL THE SMELLS

35 The breath of a young koala smells like cough drops because of the eucalyptus leaves it eats.

36 The Australian green tree frog oozes out its own insect repellant, which can smell like rotting meat, roasted cashews, or thyme leaves.

37 The star-nosed mole smells underwater by blowing out air bubbles then breathing them back in along with the scent.

38 The jewel bug may look beautiful, but when disturbed it releases an awful smell.

ALL THE SMELLS

39 The Komodo dragon can smell a dead or dying animal up to 9.5 km (5.9 mi) away.

40 A Tasmanian devil gives off a strong odour when stressed.

41 The yellow sac spider likes the smell of gasoline so much it builds its web in car engines.

COME HERE MY SWEET

42 When courting, a male great grey owl approaches a female with food in his beak. They both close their eyes as he gives her his gift.

43 The male gharial (crocodilian) attracts a mate by using the bulb-like growth at the end of his long, skinny snout to make a loud, buzzing noise and to blow water bubbles.

44 A male giant water bug does pushups in the water to attract a mate. The female, if interested, responds when she senses the waves created.

COME HERE MY SWEET

45 The tip of the male scorpion fly's tail has a pair of claspers he uses to grab a female he is interested in. He then gives her a gob of spit as a gift.

46 A male wolf spider taps his legs and mouthparts on leaves to impress a female. The better he drums, the better his chances of mating.

47 To attract a mate, the male Jamaican click beetle flies around shining a yellow-green or orange light. If the female, who remains still in a tree or bush, is interested she will shine her own light back.

48 A male goat pees on himself to attract a female.

COME HERE MY SWEET

49 When ready to mate, the female red-necked phalarope swims around a male trying to get him interested in her. After mating and laying her eggs, she abandons them all and looks for another mate.

50 The male *Jotus remus*, an Australian jumping spider, has a heart-shaped "paddle" on two of his legs. During mating season, he hides under a leaf that a female is sitting on, sticks one of his paddles up as high as he can, and waves it at her until she jumps down to check him out.

51 To attract a mate, the male red cracker butterfly makes a crackling noise that sounds like bacon frying in a pan.

COME HERE MY SWEET

52 To attract a female, the male fiddler crab waves around his extra-large, brightly coloured claw then drums rapidly on the ground with it.

53 A male walrus whistles, clacks his teeth, and makes a bell-like sound to attract a female, while floating upright in the water. If she is interested, she jumps in to to join him.

54 During courting season, the male palm cockatoo woos a female by rhythmically tapping a small branch or seedpod held in his foot against a hollow tree trunk.

55 The male balloon fly shows his interest in a female by giving her an oval-shaped silk balloon he has spun.

COME HERE MY SWEET

56 When the male short-eared owl claps his wings together as part of his courtship display, it sounds like applause.

57 A female gladiator frog is only interested in a male that can give her a nest he has either built or conquered from another male.

58 Each firefly species has a unique courtship light-flashing pattern. Some female fireflies mimic the flashing patterns of females of other species. When a male flies to her to mate, she captures and eats him instead.

LICKETY-SPLIT

59 A frog's tongue can capture prey in 0.07 second.

60 A walrus can run as fast as a human.

61 The mother-of-pearl caterpillar runs faster backward than forward.

62 A skipper butterfly can reach speeds of up to 60 km/h (37 mph).

LICKETY-SPLIT

63 A roadrunner sprints as fast as an Olympic athlete.

64 A pronghorn, the fastest North American land mammal, can reach speeds of up to 98 km/h (61 mph).

65 The tiger beetle is the fastest travelling ground insect known at 2.5 m/s (8 ft/s).

66 A star-nosed mole eats faster than any other mammal, taking 0.008 s to decide if it wants to eat something, and gobbling it down in less than 0.2 s.

OUT IT COMES

67 A crocodile cries when it eats its prey, but not because it's sad: as it eats, it huffs and hisses, forcing air through its sinuses and triggering its tear glands.

68 During a fight with a rival, a male lobster shoots pee from his bladder, which is located in his head.

69 To mark its territory, a meerkat turns the pouch on its rear end inside out—with its own unique scent—and rubs it on bushes, rocks, and other objects.

OUT IT COMES

70 When a ladybug feels threatened, it bleeds a smelly yellow liquid from its leg joints.

71 When the opossum is threatened, it plays dead and emits an odour from its rear end that smells like rotten meat.

72 A horse produces about 12 L (3 gal) of saliva each day.

73 A sloth poops only once a week, losing up to a third of its body weight each time. It never poops in a tree, where it spends most of its time, but comes down to the ground—despite the danger of predators.

OUT IT COMES

74 The violin beetle squirts out a poisonous acid when threatened.

75 The white crystals on a marine iguana's head is salt it has sneezed out that had collected in its nose glands while it was eating.

76 The kangaroo rat's pee comes out as a paste.

77 If a pupfish is unable to pass gas, it floats up to the water's surface. There it is at risk of being eaten by predators or exploding due to the pressure buildup.

OUT IT COMES

78 A wood roach nymph isn't able to digest the wood its parents eat; instead, it feeds on fluids from its parents' rear ends.

79 Octopuses, sea anemones, birds, and sloths don't pass gas.

GOING THE DISTANCE

80 The longest insect migration in the world, by dragonflies, is more than 7000 km (4350 mi) across the Indian Ocean, from India to Africa.

81 The platypus's nesting burrow can be more than 20 m (65 ft) long.

82 Over its lifetime, an arctic tern (bird) flies a distance equal to three trips to the moon and back.

GOING THE DISTANCE

83 Tryon's sea slugs sometimes travel together in single file.

84 Humpback whales have the longest migration of any mammal, travelling over 16,000 km (10,000 mi) per year.

85 When threatened, the flying fish swims straight up through the water, bursts into the air, and uses its fins like wings to glide over the water's surface—up to 200 m (650 ft)—before plunging into the ocean again.

GOING THE DISTANCE

86 A geoduck (clam) can stretch its neck 61 cm (24 in) out from its shell.

87 The flying snake launches itself from a tree and glides up to 100 m (330 ft) through the air.

88 Snow leopards can leap as far as 15 m (50 ft) in one bound.

89 The collared lizard can switch to running on its two back legs—upright like humans—when it needs to run faster.

GOING THE DISTANCE

90 The thin membrane of skin between the legs of the Southeast Asian colugo (close relative of a lemur) allows it to glide through the air up to 70 m (230 ft).

91 Koi fish can live more than 200 years.

THE BAD AND THE GOOD

92 Ambergris, which is a natural ingredient used in some of the most expensive perfumes, comes from the vomit and poop of sperm whales.

93 Although the venom of the deathstalker (a scorpion) can be life threatening, it has been used to treat brain tumours and diabetes in humans.

94 When a housefly lands on food, it spits on it to help pre-digest it. While the proteins in fly spit can spread disease, they are also used in vaccines that prevent disease.

THE BAD AND THE GOOD

95 The Gila monster's bite is venomous and painful to humans. However, its venom has been used to treat human diabetes and lung cancer.

96 The body of a caterpillar actually dissolves in its chrysalis during metamorphosis. The soupy goop then re-forms into a beautiful butterfly.

97 Large ocean-dwelling cone snails can sting and kill humans. However, their venom has been used to make drugs that treat depression, epilepsy, Parkinson's disease, and Alzheimer's.

DANCING FOOLS

98 Two male Pacific rattlesnakes do a combat dance to impress a female. They stretch up as tall as they can while swaying from side to side and then try to push each other to the ground.

99 When stopping to rest on hot desert sands, the shovel-snouted lizard rhythmically lifts alternating feet to avoid being burned to death.

DANCING FOOLS

100 The male greater sage grouse pops out the two yellow air sacs on his neck like balloons, struts, and fans his spiky tail to attract a mate.

101 A western grebe pair's mating dance starts with a side-by-side sprint together across the surface of the water, and ends with a graceful dive.

102 Two male giraffe-necked weevils battle each other with their long snouts for the right to mate with a female.

DANCING FOOLS

103 Flamingoes with the most dance moves, and the ability to switch quickly and often from one move to the other, are the most successful at finding mates.

104 When two male Galapagos Island tortoises meet during the mating season, they rise up on their front legs, stretch out their necks, and open their mouths wide. The tortoise that stretches his neck the highest wins the right to mate.

105 Male paradise riflebirds practice mating dance moves together for several years before they are ready to perform for the females.

DANCING FOOLS

106 When courting, the male red-capped manakin (bird) does a dance move that resembles Michael Jackson's "moonwalk."

107 During mating season, the male blue-footed booby (bird) does a high-stepping dance to draw attention to his bright blue feet. The brighter the blue, the healthier he is, and the more attractive he is to females.

108 Outside of courting season, an excited crane's dancing may prompt the rest of the flock to join in too.

COVERT OPERATIONS

109 The Malaysian assassin bug kills ants and then sticks them onto its back for camouflage and protection.

110 Asiatic wild dogs, which hunt in packs, communicate their plans by whistling to each other.

111 The arms of a vampire squid are connected by webbing that is black on the underside. When the squid is threatened, it draws its arms up over its body, protectively cloaking it.

COVERT OPERATIONS

112 If a weak male red-winged blackbird enters a stronger male's territory, he hides his red shoulder patches to avoid being attacked.

113 The white-winged vampire bat sneaks up on a hen and pretends to be her chick by nuzzling up to her brood patch—a featherless area on the underside of her body that appears during nesting season—then gorges on her blood.

114 The bee-eater (bird) catches a bee mid-air and removes its stinger by hitting or rubbing the bee over a hard object. It then squeezes out the bee's venom before eating it.

COVERT OPERATIONS

115 Some *Pheidole* ant larvae develop an internal organ that triggers their growth into big headed, big bodied, super soldiers whose job is to defend the colony.

116 The flat-bodied Pacific angelshark camouflages itself by lying under a thin layer of sediment on the ocean floor. When prey swims by, the shark suddenly lunges and gobbles it up.

117 When the reddish egret (bird) stands in shallow water with its wings spread, it creates a shady place where fish like to gather. It then spears its prey with its long beak.

COVERT OPERATIONS

118 A robber fly hovers at strategic locations to increase its success in ambushing prey.

119 When in danger, fire ants coordinate a counter attack against a predator by all biting and stinging at the same time.

120 The puss caterpillar looks soft and cuddly, but its long, silky hairs camouflage venomous spines.

121 Male western bluebirds battle for a territory by grabbing each other's legs. After falling to the ground they wrestle until one gets pinned. The winner pecks the loser, who then retreats.

COVERT OPERATIONS

122 The Amazonian giant centipede can capture and eat a flying bat while hanging—attached by its back end—to the roof of a cave.

123 The body, smell, and movements of the rove beetle have evolved to resemble the army ant it lives with and snacks on. It also marches with the ants on raids.

124 The "Spiderman" sea snail shoots out a mucus web to capture its prey, and then reels it in.

125 To scare predators away, one species of the *Cyclosa* spider creates a larger-than-life replica of itself using leaves, dead insects, and other debris. It then vibrates the web to make it look like the fake spider is moving.

COLOUR MY WORLD

126 The psychedelic rock gecko has a lilac body, orange tail and feet, and a yellow and green head.

127 Some grasshoppers are pink.

128 Some glass frogs have green bones.

129 The blue-footed booby gets its bright blue foot colour from pigments in the fish it eats.

130 A cutthroat trout has red-coloured slash marks on the underside of its lower jaw.

131 The Australian clusterwink snail glows a bright blue-green colour when it senses danger.

132 Reindeer eyes change from gold to blue in the winter.

133 Porcupines have orange teeth.

134 Some tarantulas are blue.

COLOUR MY WORLD

135 If a walrus gets too hot, it turns pink.

136 Crabs and octopuses have blue blood; leeches have green blood.

137 The tongue of a giraffe is bluish-black to help prevent it from getting sunburned when the giraffe sticks it out to grasp leaves.

138 The nudibranch (sea slug) occurs in a wide range of beautiful colours and patterns—from black and white to lilac to bright blue to neon pink.

139 The cream-spotted tigerwing butterfly's chrysalis is shiny gold.

140 The hickory horned devil caterpillar is green with black prickly spines and red horns.

141 Giant pandas have black skin under their black fur and pink skin under their white fur.

142 The blue-eyed black lemur is the only non-human primate that has blue eyes.

143 The tongue of the Australian blue-tongued skink is electric blue.

COLOUR MY WORLD

144 Western predatory mites are naturally white, but take on the colour of their prey for about a day after feeding.

145 Adult male botos (Amazon River dolphins) are often pink in colour.

146 The yellow tang (fish) is bright yellow during the day, but at night the colour fades as brown patches and a white horizontal band appear on its body.

147 Ladybug spots can be red, orange, yellow, black, or pink. Some ladybugs are black and white; others have stripes or checks. Some ladybugs change colour throughout the year.

OH BABY!

148 You can see the eggs of a pregnant glass frog through her skin.

149 Female guinea pigs can get pregnant at four weeks of age. They can also get pregnant again shortly after giving birth.

150 The broody squid lays up to 3000 eggs and holds the egg sac in her arms for months until hatching.

OH BABY!

151 Aphids have telescoping generations: a female carries eggs that hatch within her body, and her daughters carry eggs before they're born.

152 A female midwife toad lays her string of eggs on the male's back. He fertilizes them, then wraps the string around his legs to protect the eggs from harm.

153 The grey-brown female ostrich, which is well camouflaged during the day, gives up egg-guarding duty to the male, which has black feathers, at night.

OH BABY!

154 The fishing spider lays her eggs on a silken mat, wraps it into a ball, and carries it in her jaws until she finds the perfect place for them to hatch.

155 A female Nile crocodile sometimes rolls her eggs in her mouth to help hatch them.

156 Shortly before his mate's eggs hatch, the male Darwin's frog swallows them, storing them in the vocal sac in his throat. After the eggs hatch and the tadpoles turn into frogs–about two weeks–the male spits them out.

OH BABY!

157 After mating and laying her egg, the female emperor penguin leaves to hunt for food in the ocean. The males huddle together, each keeping his egg warm. The mothers return when the chicks hatch and take over parenting once again.

158 The female Ecuadorian horned marsupial frog carries her eggs in a pouch on her back. Each egg hatches a fully formed frog, skipping the tadpole stage.

159 An opossum is pregnant for only two weeks before her babies are born.

OH BABY!

160 Baby sawfish have a protective coating on their saws so they don't injure their mother during birth.

161 A newborn Tasmanian devil is the size of a raisin.

162 The female great white shark's eggs hatch inside her. When the babies are birthed, they immediately swim away and take care of themselves.

163 The female little brown bat hangs by her wingtips (instead of her feet) when giving birth, and catches the newborn baby with her tail.

OH BABY!

164 A newborn kangaroo can fit in a teaspoon.

165 A female North American elk hides her calf for up to 10 days after birth.

166 A baby ring-tailed lemur purrs when its mother grooms it.

167 The nine-banded armadillo almost always gives birth to identical, same-sex quadruplets.

168 A baby giant anteater spends up to a year riding on its mother's back.

169 A Korean wood-feeding cockroach nymph grows faster when raised by two parents instead of one.

170 A male sperm whale calf stays with his mother for at least four years, while a female stays with her mother for life.

171 After being separated for a short while, a mother kangaroo and her joey may kiss, hug, and groom each other when they meet again.

OH BABY!

172 When young convict cichlids (fish) return home after searching for food all day, the parents take a few at a time into their mouths and spit them out into the nest. The young fry huddle together and the adults fan them during the night.

WATER TALES

173 A jellyfish is 95% water.

174 When frightened, the porcupinefish gulps water causing its body to swell and harden and its spines to stick out. This makes it hard for predators to take a bite.

175 Some species of the blenny (fish), known as "rock hoppers," can travel short distances over land from one pool of water to another.

WATER TALES

176 The water-holding frog can survive without water during dry, hot weather by surrounding itself with its own mucus.

177 To escape predators, a dragonfly nymph squeezes its abdomen and shoots out a jet of water that propels it away.

178 Porcupines can float.

179 The violet snail floats upside down on the surface of ocean waters attached to a raft it has created of air bubbles and mucus. When it bumps into a Portuguese man-of-war, it opens its strong jaws and bites it, releasing a paralyzing purple dye.

WATER TALES

180 The ocean sunfish sunbathes by lying on its side at the surface of the water.

181 When a predator comes too close to a hoatzin (bird) chick—its nest is built on a branch over water—the chick dives into the water below. When the danger passes, the chick swims to the bank and uses the two claws found on each wing to climb back up into its nest.

182 To help it stay underwater without tipping over or floating up to the surface, a crocodile swallows stones.

183 Narwhals like to swim upside down.

WATER TALES

184 A shark swims into deeper water when it senses a hurricane coming.

185 The leatherback sea turtle can dive over 1200 m (3000 ft) below the surface of the water.

186 One teaspoon of seawater contains millions of living organisms.

187 Some bugs produce an alcohol that acts as antifreeze to stop the water in their bodies from turning to ice when it gets cold.

WATER TALES

188 Polar bears don't drink water. They get all the hydration they need from their food.

189 The electric eel can jump out of the water and surprise a predator with a high-voltage attack.

190 The larvacean builds a large mucus net around itself that traps food as it floats through mid-ocean waters. When the net gets clogged, the larvacean abandons it and builds another one. The discarded net continues to trap food as it sinks and is eaten by deep-sea animals.

COMMUNITY

191 Elephants use their trunks to comfort each other.

192 Grandmothers help raise Japanese macaque (snow monkey) young.

193 When a vampire bat that has had a successful night of hunting returns to its roost, it will regurgitate some of its food to share with those that weren't as lucky.

COMMUNITY

194 When a mother sperm whale needs to dive deep to feed, other whales protect her calf at the water's surface.

195 Cows have best friends they stick with for most of their lives.

196 When an African Matabele ant is injured, other members of its colony carry it back to their nest to take care of it.

197 A sawfly larva clusters with other larvae on the branches of eucalyptus trees for better protection from predators such as birds.

COMMUNITY

198 Four species of fish—carp, cichlid, barbel, and garra—help clean various body parts of the African hippopotamus.

199 Carpenter ants communicate by throwing up into each other's mouths.

200 Orcas work together by one pushing up on an ice floe from below so the penguins or seals fall into the water, and others capturing the prey.

201 Twenty million free-tailed bats from Mexico gather at Bracken Cave in Texas to breed—the largest gathering of mammals in the world.

202 Ermine, chimpanzee, giraffe, western scrub jay, and magpie communities all mourn when one of their own dies.

203 Female humpback whales meet up year after year–just like old friends.

204 When food is scarce, honeypot ants regurgitate the nectar they store in their abdomens for the other ants to drink.

205 The Portuguese man-of-war is actually a colony of four different polyps—none of which can survive without the other—working together as one creature.

COMMUNITY

206 When an Asian needle ant finds food that is too big to carry on her own, she returns to the nest and carries one or more sister ants, one at a time, back to the food to help.

207 The pistol shrimp and goby fish share a tunnel home dug by the shrimp. The shrimp, which has poor eyesight, keeps one of its antennae on the goby at all times. When the goby spots a predator, it signals the shrimp by flicking its tail. Then they both dash into their home.

HELPING HUMANS

208 In the waters close to Laguna, Brazil, bottlenose dolphins herd schools of fish toward waiting fishermen. The dolphins slap the water with their heads or tails to signal when the fishermen should cast their nets.

209 Capuchin monkeys are trained to help people with spinal chord injuries by turning on the television, operating a CD player, turning the pages of a book, and putting a straw into a cup for them.

HELPING HUMANS

210 Because the chemical added to natural gas to help detect leaks smells like the rotting flesh of a dead animal, a company will always investigate when they see a turkey vulture circling over a pipeline.

211 Carpenter ants have been used for thousands of years to stitch up human wounds. The ants are forced to bite and hold the edges of a wound together until it heals.

212 The greater honeyguide (bird) leads people to bee colonies so they can harvest the honey. As a reward, it gets the grubs and beeswax left behind.

HELPING HUMANS

213 Because an elephant never forgets the smell of a poacher, it can be trained to track the culprit so he or she can be caught and arrested.

214 The African giant pouched rat has a highly sensitive nose that can detect buried land mines without setting them off. It can also detect tuberculosis in human saliva.

215 The webs of golden silk orb-weavers (spiders) are so strong that fishermen in the South Pacific Ocean use them as nets for catching small fish.

HELPING HUMANS

216 Police in China use geese, which are better at alerting officers to trespassers than dogs, to aid in law enforcement.

217 Dolphins have saved drowning swimmers by lifting them up to the surface of the water.

218 Natural history museum curators use hide beetles to clean a carcass because they eat the flesh without destroying the bones.

219 Dogs use their amazing sense of smell to help locate buried victims of hurricanes, earthquakes, mudslides, and terrorist attacks.

CREATIVE/ INTELLIGENT

220 Orangutans have made whistles, rain hats, ponchos, napkins, and gloves out of leaves.

221 Sandcastle worms ooze out glue that helps them build the tube reefs they live in.

222 The giant spider crab decorates its shell with sea sponges and other deep-sea animals to camouflage it from predators.

CREATIVE/INTELLIGENT

223 The European starling adorns its nest with colourful or shiny things such as bits of plastic, scraps of paper, feathers, and coins.

224 A sand wasp flies backward slowly out of its nest so it can remember the view it must look for when it returns.

225 The male pufferfish uses his fins to create a beautiful circular design in the ocean sediment—up to 2 m (7 ft) across—to attract a mate.

226 When a yellow warbler spots a cowbird egg laid in its nest, it builds a new nest on top of the old one.

CREATIVE/INTELLIGENT

227 Termites mix their spit with sand, clay, and dung to make huge, complex homes that include food storage rooms, gardens, nurseries, the queen's chamber, tunnels, and airshafts.

228 An anteater won't fully destroy, or eat all the termites in, a nest so it can return for a meal each time the termites rebuild.

229 Raccoons can learn to pick a dozen locks in less than ten tries and repeat their feat even after the locks have been rearranged or turned upside down.

FLIP FLOP

230 A mole turns around in its narrow underground tunnel by doing a half somersault.

231 A kinkajou can rotate its ankles and feet 180° and run backwards when a predator approaches.

232 Parrotfish live in groups of many females to one male. If the male dies, one of the females changes into a male to replace him.

FLIP FLOP

233 When the razor sharp jaws of a leafcutter ant start to dull with age, it flips its job from cutting leaves to carrying leaves cut by the younger ants.

234 The giant grouper usually starts life as a female and then becomes a male if there are no or few other males in the area.

235 Flying squirrels can turn 180° in midair.

236 A tarantula hawk (spider wasp) grabs a tarantula by its rear leg, flips it over, paralyzes it with its sting, drags it into its burrow, and lays an egg on it. When the larva hatches it eats the tarantula.

FLIP FLOP

237 The chalk bass (fish) can change from male to female and back again up to 20 times a day.

238 If the hognose snake is flipped onto its front while playing dead on its back—tongue out, musky smell, and pooping—it will roll over onto its back and start its ruse all over again.

MORE THAN SKIN DEEP

239 The Bornean flat-headed frog, which has no lungs, breathes through its skin.

240 Shark skin is made up of dermal denticles, which are more like teeth than fish scales.

241 If a tiger's fur is shaved off, its stripe pattern, which is unique to each tiger, can still be seen on its skin.

MORE THAN SKIN DEEP

242 A frog usually eats the skin it sheds.

243 The skin of crocodiles that live in the rainforest caves of Gabon is bright orange because bat droppings have bleached its natural colour.

244 The stripes on a zebra protect it from insects that carry diseases. The stripes mess with an insect's vision, making it difficult for it to land.

245 A hagfish absorbs food through its skin.

MORE THAN SKIN DEEP

246 The patterns that flash across the skin of a Humboldt squid are its way of communicating.

247 A hippo oozes out reddish-brown mucus that keeps it cool, prevents bacterial infections, and protects its skin from the sun.

248 A western grebe baby has a bare patch of yellow skin on its head that turns red when it wants to be fed or when separated from its parents.

MORE THAN SKIN DEEP

249 Whales, dolphins, and porpoises all have very sensitive skin.

250 A sea otter has the thickest fur of any animal—up to 1,000,000 hairs per 6.5 cm² (1 in²) of skin.

TONGUES, MOUTHS, & TEETH

251 An aardvark's tongue is 30 cm (12 in) long.

252 The dragonfish has sharp teeth on its tongue.

253 At 8.5 cm (3.5 in) long, the tongue of the tube-lipped bat is the longest compared to body length (1.5 times) of any mammal. The tongue retracts into the bat's rib cage.

TONGUES, MOUTHS, & TEETH

254 The bowhead whale has the biggest mouth of any animal—5 m (16 ft) long by 2.5 m (8 ft) wide by 4 m (13 ft) high.

255 Sarcastic fringeheads (fish) battle over a territory by thrusting their mouths close to each other. The biggest mouth wins.

256 Kissing bugs bite humans around their mouths while they sleep.

257 A crocodile can't stick out its tongue, but an alligator can.

TONGUES, MOUTHS, & TEETH

258 During mating season, a male Emei moustache toad grows a row of spikes on its upper lips that look like a moustache.

259 A Chinese water deer has two 5 cm (2 in) long, sharp, curved upper canine teeth (tusks) sticking out from its mouth.

260 The teeth of some shark species are coated in fluoride, an ingredient found in toothpaste that prevents human tooth decay.

261 The teeth of an ocean-dwelling chiton are made of magnetite. Magnetite is not only the strongest material found in any living creature, it is also magnetic.

TONGUES, MOUTHS, & TEETH

262 A rat's front teeth can grow up to 13 cm (5 in) a year.

263 Narwhal males rub their tusks (long teeth) together to communicate.

264 The suckers on a squid's arms and tentacles are lined with teeth made from chitin, a substance similar to that which forms human fingernails.

265 A dolphin keeps the full set of teeth it was born with throughout its life. Because its teeth have growth rings, a dolphin's age can be estimated by counting the rings, similar to what is done with a tree.

IF TREES COULD TALK

266 The grey fox is the only member of the North American canine family that can climb trees.

267 During the day, the common potoo (bird) sits still in a tree disguised as a tree branch.

268 The coconut crab, which has a leg span of up to 1 m (39 in), can climb a palm tree and cut down a coconut with its strong pincers. After climbing back down, it cracks open the coconut and gorges on the food inside.

IF TREES COULD TALK

269 Black bearded saki monkeys never sleep in the same tree two nights in a row.

270 A tree-dwelling frog found in Ecuador has a claw on the side of its thumb that it uses to fight predators and other males.

271 A Wallace's giant bee feeds tree resin to its young.

272 During nesting season, the female knobbed hornbill (bird) seals the entrance to her nest—found in a hole in a tree—using a paste made of chewed food and poop. She then makes a small slit in the seal through which the male passes food for his family, and through which she poops.

IF TREES COULD TALK

273 The green algae that grow on the slow-moving sloth help camouflage it in the trees where it lives.

274 The great grey shrike mimics the call of a bird to attract a member of that species, then captures and impales it on a sharp tree branch or thorn.

275 The slender mudskipper (fish) can climb steep inclines like trees and rock faces to find food or to sunbathe.

276 Wood ducks, buffleheads, common goldeneyes, common mergansers, and hooded mergansers are all water birds that nest in trees.

IF TREES COULD TALK

277 The underside of the Indian oakleaf butterfly looks like a dead leaf.

278 Mormon crickets usually eat plants, but sometimes they eat each other.

279 If the common walkingstick falls off a plant during the day, it will lie still until it's dark, then slowly climb back up.

280 The aye-aye (primate) of Madagascar uses its extra-long middle finger to tap on hollow trees. When it hears insects or larvae disturbed by the taps moving around, it bites through the tree and uses its long finger to pull the prey out.

TOXIN TALES

281 Venom from ant bites and bee stings have been used to power fuel cells for small devices such as cell phones and digital cameras.

282 The iguana lizard can break off its tail when a snake bites it to prevent the venom from spreading to the rest of its body.

283 The bulldog ant's venomous sting can kill a human within 15 minutes.

TOXIN TALES

284 The saddleback caterpillar is covered with spines that inject venom into any creature that brushes against it.

285 The venom of the horned viper contains over a dozen different toxins.

286 The 5 cm (2 in) golden poison frog has enough venom in it to kill ten men.

287 A box jellyfish has thousands of toxic stinging cells on its tentacles. Its venom is so painful that human victims can die of heart failure before getting to shore, or go into shock and drown.

TOXIN TALES

288 When a fire ant covers a crazy ant with its toxic venom, the crazy ant smears its own acid over its body to neutralize it.

289 The black-headed grosbeak (bird) can eat monarch butterflies, which are toxic to most birds.

290 The female jewel wasp stings a cockroach and injects it with venom in the part of the brain that controls movement. After chewing off half of each antenna, she leads the cockroach to her burrow where she lays her egg on its abdomen. When the larva hatches, it feeds on the cockroach.

TOXIN TALES

291 Some rough-skinned newts carry enough poison to kill several adult humans. However, the common garter snake has developed a resistance to its venom, making it the only known animal today that can eat this newt and survive.

292 The hooded pitohui (bird) is not only toxic to the touch it gives off a nasty smell.

293 The toxin found in the wing tips of the great orange tip butterfly is identical to the toxin found in the marbled cone snail, which lives in the ocean.

BY THE NUMBERS

294 A loggerhead sea turtle can hold its breath underwater for up to four hours.

295 A desert locust swarm can cover 1200 km² (463 mi²), with 40 to 80 million locusts occupying each square kilometer.

296 The greater wax moth hears 150 times better than humans.

BY THE NUMBERS

297 Giraffes in the wild sleep as little as 30 minutes a day—the least of any mammal.

298 The ocean sunfish can produce up to 300 million eggs at a time.

299 Male pectoral sandpipers fly up to 12,800 km (8000 mi) over a month's time to mate with as many females as possible.

300 Greenland sharks can live more than 500 years.

BY THE NUMBERS

301 The average adult Canada goose poops about 0.9 kg (2 lbs) a day.

302 The largest Atlantic manta ray ever recorded had a 9.1 m (30 ft) wide wingspan.

303 A blue whale's heart beats 8 to 10 times per minute; an Etruscan shrew's heart beats up to 1511 times per minute.

304 The record for the largest number of fish held in an Atlantic puffin's bill is 61.

BY THE NUMBERS

305 Sharks go through as many as 30,000 teeth in their lifetime.

306 The midge flaps its wings over 62,000 times per minute.

307 A typical bed mattress has between 100,000 and 10 million dust mites.

308 Regardless of their shape or size, most mammals take about 12 seconds to poop.

THAT'S JUST NOT RIGHT

309 Newly hatched praying mantis nymphs sometimes eat their siblings.

310 Ravens crush ants and rub them all over their bodies as an insect repellent and/or to soothe their skin during molting.

311 A sea star forces the shell of its prey open using the strong suction of its tube feet, pushes its stomach out through its mouth, inserts it into the opening, breaks down the shellfish's body with digestive juices, and absorbs the food into its stomach.

THAT'S JUST NOT RIGHT

312 The moray eel can tie its body into knots to squash its food so it is easier to swallow.

313 A male giraffe drinks the pee of a female while she's peeing to tell if she's ready to mate.

314 Adult members of the Dracula ant colony chew holes in their larvae and suck out their blood without killing them.

315 The parasitic jaeger (seabird) steals food from other birds, or bullies birds that have just eaten until they throw up. It then eats the bird's vomit.

THAT'S JUST NOT RIGHT

316 The oldest unborn sand tiger shark in a pregnant female's womb eats its unborn siblings.

317 The female goliath bird-eating spider will sometimes eat her partner after mating.

318 The larva of a hunchback fly climbs up a spider's leg, gnaws a hole in its body, climbs in, and lives in the spider feeding on its insides.

319 A baby caecilian (snake-like amphibian) feeds by peeling off and eating bits of its mother's outer layer of skin.

THAT'S JUST NOT RIGHT

320 Some praying mantises eat birds, starting with their brains.

321 The slender loris (primate) rubs its pee over its hands, face, and feet to protect itself against the stings of the toxic beetles and cockroaches it feeds on.

322 An egg-eating snake uses its neck bones to crack open an egg it has swallowed whole. The contents of the egg are squeezed out and eaten, and the shell is regurgitated.

323 A cookiecutter shark feeds on round chunks of flesh it bites off other fish, mammals, and even humans.

THAT'S JUST NOT RIGHT

324 A giraffe cleans its nose and ears with its tongue.

325 If the Port Jackson shark eats something its body is unable to digest, it turns its stomach inside out and spits the offending material out of its mouth.

326 To protect itself when a predator threatens, the hairy frog breaks its own toe bones to create a set of retractable claws that poke through its skin like the Marvel Comics character Wolverine.

327 A dead jellyfish can still sting you.

YOU CAN'T MAKE THIS STUFF UP

328 Slave-making ants steal the young from nests of other ants and raise them as slaves.

329 Scientists have been able to show through CT scanning that an adult butterfly can remember things that happened to it when it was a caterpillar.

330 The arowana (fish) can jump up to 2 m (6.6 ft) out of the water to catch small birds or insects resting on overhanging branches.

331 Bat hair was once used as money.

332 The bat-eared fox's hearing is so good it can hear the eggs of beetles buried underground hatch.

333 When a giant water bug senses a flash flood about to happen, it crawls out of the stream and up the bank to escape. When the danger is over, it returns to the water.

334 When threatened, the swell shark curls around to hold its tail fin in its mouth and sucks in water, making it balloon out and difficult for predators to bite.

335 A capybara is a giant rodent—almost as tall as a German shepherd—that lives in the rainforests, flooded savannas, and wetlands of South America.

336 African elephants are afraid of bees.

337 A meerkat eats a venomous scorpion by biting off its stinger and brushing any remaining venom off the scorpion's body, before dining on it.

338 Birds can't taste the chemical compound found in chili peppers that makes a human feel like his or her mouth is on fire.

339 When danger threatens, the South African girdled lizard jams itself into a crack in a rock and inflates its body so it's impossible to remove.

340 A female manatee's nipples are found in her armpits.

341 The male proboscis monkey's nose is normal size at birth. As the monkey matures, his nose grows so large that it ends up hanging down over his lips.

342 After the caterpillar of the Ross's metalmark butterfly hatches from its egg, wood ants take it to their underground nest and care for it so they can harvest the sugary honeydew it oozes from its hind legs.

343 Arctic jellyfish are found under polar ice.

344 The blind, white, ghost slug kills earthworms with its razor-sharp teeth, then sucks them up like spaghetti.

345 Tawaki penguins live in the rainforests of New Zealand.

346 After mating, a female cactus bee uses her head to drill a nesting hole in the soil, into which she carves about a dozen cells. She puts a lump of nectar mixed with pollen in each cell, lays an egg, and seals each cell. Then she dies from exhaustion.

347 Wasps sometimes pick up ants and move them to another location so they don't have to compete with them for the same food.

348 When danger approaches a field cricket couple, the male lets the female run into the burrow before he does.

349 Some kinds of piranhas are vegetarian.

350 Goats have been genetically engineered to produce milk that contains spider silk. When the goat is milked, the silk is separated out and used to make bulletproof vests or artificial tendons.

351 The female anglerfish has a spine sticking out of her head just above her mouth that looks like a fishing pole with a lighted lure.

352 Honeybees have been trained to solve basic math problems.

353 The red-lipped batfish, which has a bright red mouth and a horn on its head that houses a lighted lure, walks on the ocean floor with its fins.

354 Maremma sheepdogs protect a colony of the world's smallest penguins from predators on a small island off the coast of Victoria, Australia.

355 The markings on the back of a shield bug found in Singapore looks like the face of a man with a pompadour hairstyle.

356 The egg case of the Port Jackson shark looks like a corkscrew.

357 The Antarctic blackfin icefish's blood is nearly transparent, and its bones are so thin you can see its brain through its skull.

358 The female sea spider's legs contain her eggs and her digestive system.

359 The sooty grouse (bird) spends most of its time in the winter eating the needles of coniferous trees.

360 The Chinese mitten crab has furry claws that look like mittens.

361 An electric eel uses jolts of electricity to disable a fish's muscles—similar to how a Taser gun works—before sucking it into its mouth.

362 The giant squid has a bagel-shaped brain. Because its esophagus (food pipe) runs through the hole, it must tear its prey into small pieces or it will damage its brain while it eats.

363 To escape a predator, the chevrotain (mouse deer) dives underwater and stays on the bottom, sometimes tethered to a plant or reed, for up to four minutes until the danger passes.

364 Crows prefer fries in a bag with a McDonald's logo to ones in a plain paper bag.

365 The vampire spider is the only creature known to choose prey based on what its prey has eaten: female mosquitoes that have just gorged themselves on human blood.

See how many you can answer without looking back! Answers are on p. 117.

1. What bird's eyes are bigger than its brain?

2. What are three reasons the male Madagascar hissing cockroach might hiss?

3. What male creature gives the gift of a gob of spit to a female he likes?

4. What is the fastest-eating mammal?

5. What creature shoots pee from his head when he fights?

6. What four-legged creature can run on its two back legs when it wants to run extra-fast?

7. What does a male blue-footed booby do to attract a mate?

8. What does the Amazonian giant centipede snack on while hanging down from the roof of a cave?

9. What colour are porcupine teeth?

10. What animal rolls her eggs in her mouth to help them hatch?

11. What tiny creature is used to help stitch wounds on humans?

12. What male fish creates a beautiful design in the ocean sediment to attract a mate?

13. What does a frog do with the skin it sheds?

14. What does the common potoo disguise itself as?

15. What large mammal is afraid of bees?

1. Ostrich (#6).
2. To sound an alarm, when fighting another male, and to attract a female (#28).
3. Male scorpion fly (#45).
4. Star-nosed mole (#66).
5. Male lobster (#68).
6. Collared lizard (#89).
7. He does a high-stepping dance (#107).
8. Bat (#122).
9. Orange (#133).
10. Nile crocodile (#155).
11. Carpenter ant (#211).
12. Male pufferfish (#225).
13. Eats it (#242).
14. Tree branch (#267).
15. African elephant (#336).

AUTHOR'S NOTE

The information contained in this book was researched and verified with the most reliable and up-to-date resources possible. Primary and secondary sources included scholarly papers, scientific journals, newspapers, magazines, books, documentaries, videos, and websites. However, the field of science is ever changing, and what may be accepted as fact today may be discarded tomorrow as new knowledge surfaces. I have done my very best to bring you the most accurate tidbits of information at the time of publication.

PRAISE FOR
When Crocodiles Cry:
365 MORE AMAZING FACTS ABOUT THE ANIMAL KINGDOM

"What an incredible collection of intriguing, obscure animal facts! Middle-years students will enjoy this information, voiced in vivid and entertaining ways. It will enhance anyone's interest in, and understanding of, the animal world."

– Alison Lohans, award-winning author
of 27 books for young people including
Caught in the Crossfire (Pearson Education Australia, 2019),
No Place for Kids (Heritage House, 2014),
and *Picturing Alyssa* (Dundurn, 2011)

"Be prepared to be dazzled with fascinating and fun facts about the animal kingdom. Have your curiosity sparked, and your funny bone tickled by this delightful second collection gathered from Sally Meadows' remarkable research. These intriguing details are sure to impress even the keenest mind."

-Judith Silverthorne,
award-winning author

"Like the first book in this series, *When Sleeping Birds Fly: 365 Amazing Facts About The Animal Kingdom*, this volume is chock full of delightful and surprising information and should be in every home and school library – anywhere curious minds can be found!"

-Tracy Krauss,
award-winning author, educator,
and curriculum consultant

"I live in a world where it's too easy to forget that nature is always out there waiting to be discovered. *When Crocodiles Cry* is just what we need to remind us how surprising and awesome the animal kingdom is. Sally Meadows' book left me saying, 'Wow!'"

-Brenda Baker,
award-winning author
and children's entertainer

"*When Crocodiles Cry*, like *When Sleeping Birds Fly*, is full of amazing and interesting facts that are sure to whet the curiosity of young and old alike. Read it in its entirety, or enjoy it one category at a time, one fact at a time! Looking forward to the next book in this *365 Amazing Facts* series!"

**-Deborah McConkey,
teacher-librarian**

"Sally Meadows has done it again with the second book in her series, *When Crocodiles Cry: 365 More Amazing Facts About The Animal Kingdom*. She has provided us with a fun read full of even more bizarre animal stats that are sure to wow the reader. *When Crocodiles Cry* engages students and adults alike, and is a great diving board from which to plunge into further knowledge. The organization, font, and short, tasty tidbits of obscure facts, add up to make this a delightful title for any bookshelf."

**-Rhonda Morari,
retired teacher-librarian**

ALSO BY THE AUTHOR

*When Sleeping Birds Fly:
365 Amazing Facts About
The Animal Kingdom*

The Underdog Duckling

The Two Trees

Beneath That Star

COMING SOON!

*When Sleeping Birds Fly
For The Creative Soul*

*When Jellyfish Rain From The Sky:
365 Amazing Facts About
The World Around Us*

To keep up with all her news,
sign up for Sally's newsletter at
https://sallymeadows.com.

Sally Meadows is an award-winning Canadian author, singer-songwriter, and speaker. A former scientist, children's entertainer, and educator, Sally is passionate about sharing amazing science facts with curious readers of all ages. This is her fifth book.

You can connect with Sally at

    https://sallymeadows.com

    sally@sallymeadows.com

    https://instagram.com/sallymeadowsmusic

    https://www.facebook.com/SallyMeadowsMusic

    https://twitter.com/SallyMeadows

www.ingramcontent.com/pod-product-compliance
Lightning Source LLC
Chambersburg PA
CBHW060403080526
44583CB00012B/443